if: prey,
then: huntress

if: prey, then: huntress

CHRISTINA SHAH

1 2 3 4 5 — 29 28 27 26 25

Nightwood Editions
P.O. Box 1779
Gibsons, BC V0N 1V0
Canada
www.nightwoodeditions.com

TYPOGRAPHY: Rafael Chimicatti

Nightwood Editions acknowledges the support of the Canada Council for the Arts, the Government of Canada, and the Province of British Columbia through the BC Arts Council.

Canada Council for the Arts
Conseil des Arts du Canada

This book has been printed on 100% post-consumer recycled paper.

Printed and bound in Canada.

LIBRARY AND ARCHIVES CANADA CATALOGUING IN PUBLICATION
Title: If: prey, then: huntress / Christina Shah.
Other titles: If: prey, then: huntress (Compilation)
Names: Shah, Christina, author.
Identifiers: Canadiana (print) 20250225360 | Canadiana (ebook) 20250225387 |
ISBN 9780889715028 (softcover) | ISBN 9780889715035 (EPUB)
Subjects: LCGFT: Poetry.
Classification: LCC PS8637.H3482 I4 2025 | DDC C811/.6—dc23

For Paul

CONTENTS

In nova fert animus mutatas dicere formas/corpora
(I intend to speak of forms changed into new entities)
—Ovid, *Metamorphoses, Book 1*

wave pool

birdgirls in bikinis take flight,
chlorine Icarians
arms wide, caught by laughing men
one-third submerged

green screed on
weisswurst torsos
monkey puzzle pectoral definition
twentysomething dendrites
struck lightning on young fathers' chests

mothers hide abscission striations
with zebra induced impressionism
or flowered rebellion—
heavy cleavage a diversion and a reminder
in a pained tankini

teenage boys drop as depth charges
knowing, lanky aerodynamicists
in the deep end

teal neon slapdashes alternate above
a herd of plastic chairs; argon warns that
THIS IS A WAVE POOL

interior bar, 1986

imagine boom, echo. your
underground father emerges
into a lean-to town
Ansel Adams' anticlines
bungalows and gasfoodlodging;
concrete cats crawling at their ankles

twin falls, one tavern. that men's den.
gold dust woman on dirty checkerboard
feathers, slipped fins flap
stiff on tanned hips
Eagles' epode warns sailors.

like you can move within a trap.

crew splices near misses with not a chance,
table populated with empties
butts with the wind knocked out of 'em.
he's dreaming she's Pegasus

she's mining time in grams

XXX

Saturn returns
just as the snooze button sticks,
listing to starboard atop beta waves.
a meditative young man shakes you awake,
thinking you are a keeper of nightstand arcana.

his words are spilled gasoline—
you're hitting your peak, he says,
and suddenly you smell of sandalwood and musk,
and you realize you need to dress better.
your half-smile is a pulled thread, puckering your self's seam
as you silently implode with the reminder.

you hold a funeral for the sound and fury of the twenties,
mourn how many times you gave yourself up and away,
allowing this youthful ambergris to float off
into your choppy grey subconscious.

Britannia Mine

for Peter Babiak

I knew you when you were down and dirty.

you wore corrugated dungarees;
leaned against the mountain
hip cocked against Howe Sound
like a pink lady, smokin' away.

the young Italian Teamsters
beamed when they heard your name—
their grandfathers
built their piece of the New World
in your belly,
breaking rock with
bad English

I'm no Jonah,
but later I got under your skin
and took your azurite pulse
with one damp finger

orogenic junkie
that I am
your ore-cart's track marks
still ladder my forearms
I'm busted, but I've still got
diamond-star drillholes in my veins

what am I now?
withdrawn and feverish
and what are you now,
you shining, electroplated ghost?

check out your fake tits:
a yoga studio,
soft-serve
and made-in-China native trinkets
for the cubicle tourists
visiting the gift shop for the motor of the world
with no memory of being born of Vulcan's forge—
the guilty, divorced from the nature of things

on their iPads, whose axons are fashioned from your bones

noble gas town

fifties glow sticks
rigidly lit Chinatown's shoulders
chandelier earrings
dangled above
its peasant dress,
its seamy selvedge
befitting a young port city

Las Vegas of the north,
krypton promising
mid-century sin, fun
at the edge of the earth

bamboo terrace's xenon fronds
Smilin' Buddha's neon chop suey alphabet
made bloody watercolours
on bleary streets

Foo's ho ho,
Ming's pictograms glowed,
blew kisses at passers-by—
their starlit Formica runways
palm their universal balm—
bowls of noodle soup
whose dumpling islands
invited the nighthawks in

jerrycan crawl

Saturday morning;
a broken mirror to
an unstable temporal lobe.

you took my hand just as you
ran out of gas.
the walk in search of momentum
was the story of your
rock garden,
and you admired my printmaking
on broken earth
bordered by backhoe rickrack.

the city's new metal hyphae—
a nod to construction's coarse-grained markers:
meshed penitentiary,
steel CN filaments and
concrete fascia of the Living Hope church

you tell me about religion as categorized
on dog tags
you tell me how you are to hide
the vital lies in your mouth
should you ever go down.

Scott

the young sheet metal shapeshifter
jerks his hoodie aside
to show the shitheel marks
copyright symbols hunted and pecked
along the smooth dunes of his neck and back
by the weekend's one-hit wonder
now scattered two provinces over.

she was a BC girl; you're a BC girl, he says
like it's some fine-grained terroir,
like I might be more.
so sure he could show me a thing or two
despite my five fingers of life's wringer on him.

this barroom Dante displays a harlequined calf,
imprinted damnation
of his own design.

the man is night-blind.
I am just the ferry captain
with a liquor gun to steer this rickety room;
thin solace in low-rise jeans.

Paul

you were
a hewer

now a whetter
of balsam minds
through foreign mirrors
mokume-gane to the morning assembled
before you

kids these days don't know
sinew and burled bone
your arms, still
smooth-talking cousins
to those choked pines

now they answer you back
pulp, inked and bound
shelved flush; the bricks of your hermitage
on your return
as the Diogenes of your bright harbour

looking for an honest man
line by line

bra

dashed on the unshaven couch
lace wings thrown open, exhausted
a jalousie yawning on a blinding morning
doubled-over hooked tongues and square eyes—
a casualty of man's practised dexterity
on the teen spirit rosary

a diorama with such promise
of soft lunar dunes

a splaying of beige plique-à-jour
over blush polyamide cups—
cups that invite the warmth of palms
and lips

this strange vestige
of Victorian corsetry
with its crude wiring—
a mammarian sling
a mastic dam
waiting to bust
after eight taut hours
or one hot instant

snoring

apnea's gap—
a growling glottal stop.
then tongue tumbles back
into the palate's crevasse

exasperated, his spouse can't take this
passed-out rasping in her ear,
carotid zydeco of his breath's seized engine,
this thoracic panic

it's late-night exile
from satin to sweaty leather
he leaves her curling warm bum
for the solitary lolling sprawl

pinky laundry

their dirty custard ranks
present a row of grooved tongues crooked
for a six-quarter shakedown
with a thin rinse

pregnant, trembling, spinning
boxing bloodied socks and jeans
punishing the textile transgressions
of poor days dodged

into the side-gyre
mesh drum tumbling
hot chaos rising in five-minute increments

here, we're our own hunchbacked bellmen
wheeling our low-slung carts
below entombed fluorescent bars
Charons ferrying terrycloth,
folding the rabbled souls.

dear Rudyard

Well, the twain met—
not at the gates of Vienna
nor on a date at the Prater,
but in an artificial city
by Trudeaumanic accident.

I learned to make killer Vanillekipferln—
blond almond dust and cultured butter,
gorgeous orchid's wizened finger buried
in bright sand to disperse
migration's black grains.

I learned to consume my mezzaluna origins
in time for Midnight Mass—
marvel at the old man's Sunday absences;
the porcine avoidance
of his distant past.

sky dynes

Picasso's donkey hits the dirt on the downswing—
this ride screams for us,
scaly yellow isosceles skeleton
straining under the play of
bare feet flat against elms' veils;
seed-dispersal parachute souls
blown beyond the alchemy of palms and iron plaits,
past the canvas barquettes of these gluteal galleons.

a little mottled dog sits clear of the sandpit,
blasé as he watches us razz gravity.

Spanish Banks

few city beach burners
venture into the estuary
without inflatable toys
or big boy shotgun versions

we, however, teeter as ocean pedestrians
over unseen barnacle carbuncles
underfoot

then plunge, flail freely
in the brisk weak saline
rake seaweed with fingers
imagine our mermaid plaits

bathers made micro
by freighters
waiting for berth or barge

look back at the glass stacks
of the urban squeeze

lie back, float
forget chairs
and their imperatives—
and whip-kick
the evening

the Afghan man

the Afghan man
has eight canine
Farrah Fawcett marionettes—
some blondes and brunettes
radiating from the inside-out
umbrella skeleton of straps.

they fall into a Lido shuffle
and sashay down the cobblestone catwalk.

which?
rich?
bitch?

what sofa set needs protection
from your afternoon of indiscretion?
where is the soignée divorcée
who warrants your attention?

one can never be too sure
if the girls miss her,
as the man with the unerring eye
extracts the garrulous burrs
that starfuck their fur.

*pep!*tization

gelid.
change of state
hot tartaric crystals
congeal to cool semisolid colloid
to slurpable lipidless Jell-O.

queasy green giggle ziggurat
entombed in its amber Pyrex bungalow
mollifying the elderly,
the indolent,
the jailed.

bad soup

it's the mirage in the cold Gobi
you crawl stiffly towards it—sick, exhausted;
anticipating its rich heat and your satiety
its motherly hug banishing the rain shadow

it's a gut punch—
worse than sand in the Vaseline
broth that leans on the horn
bleached greens
eroding tofu
occasional vermicelli filaments
cartilaginous pork sliced, recoiling like the
frayed flags of failed states
a raw egg becomes a heavy nova,
forming a thousand rubber microbeads

prawn brains explode onto your hands

your spectral server
slips you a ploughman's solid bill
and does not even extrude a gelatinous
thank you

seafood department

Neptune's flesh linens—
filleted billet-doux
displayed under clingfilm
on stainless steel gallery shelves

pictures of the floating world

Styrofoam futons, dormitory-style
their studded, extruded blue spoom
does not hint at ichythyosaurian history

carp's branded scales
a bleeding irezumi iron street grate

array of baby octopus
cartilaginous little baseball mitts

dressed smelts—prophets
gleaming in mass graves

prawn

dendrobranchiata
you throw your roe out
like you remove a cava cage
spill the wine, let life flow
into its briny flute

you arrive already beheaded for us Westerners,
we peel your exoskeletal armour
plate by plate and
reveal your cloudy muscularity,
your silver and black decapod's
slumped magnetic record

your black inner tube gutted
with a sperm whale zip letter opener
as some poop chute party trick

the perfect chameleon
until you assume your firm fetal curl
on the lemon wedge penthouse sectional

a cooked
naked pink
cowering windsock

prosciutto

lipid ribbons.
microplaned layers piled,
stripped of anatomical gravity,
pork's loose locks
swept up off life's nape,
pulled taut at the end of its long arm—
half that tight dance with
the vine's blood, its astringent echo
of pepper, flesh, flower.

fettuccine all'uovo N° 94 (the carbonara poem)

our pasts lay desiccated
tangled pasta nests
in glassine windows

waiting to be saline,
salient, pliable grist

as coal miners we emerge from black dust;
you add the rendered events

rough-cut jowl
and the Pecorino Romano
of umami's imperfect memory

and make fat silk threads

potato jacket (community garden)

young spuds—soft snakeskins
not yet leathery, cynic-eyed
the grower wraps clay-jewelled potatoes
in a jean jacket furoshiki
a hobo n00b, his Zippo
and some tawny tobacco shag
fall back into black earth

Ukrainian Orthodox Christmas

for Norman and Gerry

already we are January anacondas
resembling dromedaries.
lying inert
on what the eastern oldsters call
the chesterfield
booze and consumer debt hangovers
ebbing eventually

but
not
so
fast.

one more dinner with the in-laws
for the duodenal drop-of-doom

the long table, the tired burro
Perun's signs stitched on traditional linen
protection from lightning
(as for heartburn, you're on your own)

waxing moon perogies perspiring
spareribs with their frizzy sauerkraut toupees
in their chafing dish test pattern.
magenta borscht percolating
anticipating the cool sour cream torpedo

and of course, a special thanks to Mrs. Vilve Yachke—
for once again providing the cabbage rolls and the coffee

man, not even vodka will give us liftoff tonight

asparagus

spring's sentries
shrill with chlorophyll
rubber-banded phalanxes
fill farmers' market stalls
adolescent stalks
spindly impudent spears
with their scaly fauxhawks
those rebel yells out in force—
the first sign winter has lost the fight

or, echoing snow,
arrive deliberately albino—
inexplicably bunkered
by exuberant Germans
sparkling over April's *Weißspargel*,
then shipped out in glass cylinder galleries
stolid in citric lymph
aching for a hollandaise duvet

banana

scabby banana
stickerless, untraceable
slowly becoming time-dappled
like sun worshippers who bake
despite the warnings

an odd stunt double
for cocks and guns

a finger detached from its hand
with a dark political backstory

a fast fashion shakedown
an epithet
and worse—
ridiculous gonch

it has its own class of accessories:
hangers, slicers and
protectors resembling giant clown harmonicas

under its thick shearling jacket
white gold pegged with black potassium pinpoints

the hangover boomerang

ice cream cones

wielding the steel scoop,
a teenage girl directs
the only acceptable conversation
on sensual pleasure—
rolled and doled out into a crisp, gridded
contrapuntal little envelope

marbled orbs form from fantasy
black cherry galaxies
pistachio asteroids

nothing like being too old
to make out on the corner
walking down the street on a hot evening,
kids see us and want to be us,
paunchy and holding hands, staid and stately

circumnavigating the Milky Way
with our tongues

autumn meditation

splendid death's
ombré sweeps trees
a golden slowhand burn
crackling desiccation
(leaf blowers howling
EVERY FUCKING WEDNESDAY)
then fungal flowering
people turn to spices
and squashes
in sweataweatha
get serious
mourn August's
endless possibilities
its stone fruit
and cool lakes
its hot pink toenails

gel nails

every three weeks
the new keratin carapace
slides the old opalescence
forward, shifting the lithosphere

the tips experience
chips, incursions
from relentless encounters
with life's fine motor requests

the new moon is
trying to rise ten times over—
albino and pliable
in its pink spatulate bed

under the gel shelf
real girl grain—
calcium galaxies
fungal rebellion
hangnails calling
at all hours

the tech drills
sparkles to space dust
files and drywalls
the back gaps:
the binocular work of
microindustrial beauty

the conversation filters into the ditch
between two worlds
as one smoky plum-glazed hand
cures in its ultraviolet drive-in

botulinum toxin

the dentist's sideshow
the home canner's cold sweat

spoiling poison rods are revealed,
flooded with crystal violet

it's the microbial tightrope walker
lurking in the dirt,

waiting to pervert ferments
or erase faces

for that refreshed look

your guitar

six butterflied thumbs
six mystery steel ligaments

you try to explain domino frets to me
but I am an abandoned pianist
raised on eighty-eight teeth

mired in anxiety
at my childhood recital

you can embrace its fat butternut body
its brindled blond wood
wherever you go

elicit its secret history
with your soft hands

the keytar's lament

I can't get no respect.
synth sphinx—fabulous creature of the musical zoo,
preserve of feathered-hair bands
the weaker members wank and *wah*
on my slippery plastic phalanges
in search of a good time and an easy ride

people snort my name
bastard-child lumped in with tangelos and pluots—
hybrids no one buys

I've never had a full-time gig
at least I'm big in Japan
"shoulder keyboard" they call me, reverently,
without a sliver of irony—
bathroom tissue instead of toilet paper.

I dream of a home
where I'm rockin'
my red lacquered skin,
my trapezoid torso a popstar parade sash—
my squishy polyphonic giggles burbling forth

elegy for a plastic bag

your role's over
gymnastic plastic
once slippery and lithe,
paper's saviour
now varicose

this useless afterlife
reviled
turning fugu pirouettes
counting headlights on the highway
gnashing chain-link by the airport

shame of the grocery run
now the baleen's bane—

baled in a foreign grave

brain cactus

you slow-glowing dream
under fruit and flower light

echinopsis eclipsing the limits
of its sit-tight plastic

smell-less
cerebellar and stellar

its mechanical crenulation
a traumatic reticulation

verdant curvilinear crevasses
in their crust of dirt and perlite

radiant peridot wrinkles spark
tiny spines that form satellite stars

a freak that asks for nothing
in thin winter

you beautiful cancer—
mutant that will never bloom

x-ray clinic

sunflower walls
and pretend pine chairs
could be a Montessori school
could be a Polish deli—
take a number and they'll see to
your meat and bones

it's standing room only for medical imagists
folks in their winter darks
staring at the electronic eye in their hands

the old man next to me smells like piss,
confirmed by the carbamide sunrise on his crotch
yet seems to grasp texting well—
internal ping pong occurs
as there's nowhere else to sit

the radiographer has me drape
a giant lead apron in my lap,
as if at some dystopian lobster fest
and make tinman shadow puppets
the headcrusher gesture
and sign language—
the letter *f* on the cassette runway

the laser's thin red line sprints
across my knuckles
my hand, a jammed fan

wedding ring steadfastly
refusing the evacuation order

ulnaris/radialis

egret, backhoe—
hand origami's
carpal puppetry
prepares her for
the works and days
of women:
beery neon trays,
Electrolux™ espaliers
and 55 wpm.

3–6

happy hour—
the clay layer oasis between
work's late heavy bombardment
and the domestic cooling trend

fissure

this time, you drive

into the concrete stress,
in your blue dress shirt,
going downtown on coffee and vitriol—
today, I am a tourist in your life

we glide in, stop illegally
at the law's glass plaza,
with its living boxwood stole
draped across its storied shoulders

here we are, at that hill of crosses
where everyone gets what's theirs

wrenches rest—
today, your words are
the dancer in a minefield
of vesiculated memories

you face the lava
bleeding into the chop
your marriage stays viscous, rhyolitic
she's psychic snail gel
peeling the paint off life's ledge—
reeling registered letters through the years

her counsel examines the cracks in your undersea pilings
not knowing you are a hairline barophile

brindled with gold

trade show

this is no place for the noctambulant. everyone files into the convention hall at nine, phones effervescing—all cologne and the newest mitered shoes, nipped pants. chalky scones and anemic coffee are put out to pasture in the back corner. a swag-o-rama arrayed at each dirndled booth—sexy lanyards, polyester golf tees that cling to nipples and spare tires in July. use a mnemonic to remember Rob/Randy/Raj. wax on about whatever you've got—piston pumps, software-as-perpetual-subscription, or the easy three-star resort you hauled your carcass to in February. Puerto Vallarta—reliable if anything. such a peachy keynote—if you're going to bore them, bog them down with bar charts while they're still waking up. competitors slink by, proffer side-eye and the occasional polite broadside, as hey, we're all pretend friends here. cross your fingers and keep your spine straight as your arches fall, all Lomanesque on ambition's thin carpet. mingle like a free radical. then toast the round of friends for your drinks at four.

inventory

part numbers murmured as
evening vespers by the paid faithful

warehouse calisthenics—
coworkers crouching to see
what sprockets lurk along lower shelves—
ancient cast-iron catfish
bottom-feeding

straining to reach overstock
abandoned haplessly
ten feet up

counting safety wands nested
into giant neon dildoes
while Dan is talking to himself in aisle B03

Friday evening is far from over
and corporate has cast fried chicken
upon the waters

mice—migrants from the casino next door drop in
and we sincerely hope the stateside auditor
does not spot them

who fucked this up? someone mutters
disturbing the dust
among a myriad of greased bearings
stainless steel lifesavers in a tube

an explosion of work gloves
with meathead superhero names
like *dogfight* and *stealth*

for saving yourself from yourself
when you slip
with the boxcutter

vending machine blues

cement dust—this industrial frost
covers every surface
of the jammed, damned
yard vending machine
call me Ishma-HAL, it taunts—
an IT moai whose touchscreen
displays a delphic error code

one wheel in the ditch
you call Alabama
hang yourself in its telephone tree
half an hour later a software reset:
they port in, code cascading
in pixelating prayer
straight from *The Matrix*

no dice.
no gods in the machine
the plastic carousel grinds,
straitjacketed by unseen occlusions
within its rotating catacombs
perhaps the crisp wrapper
for a pair of safety glasses
or a cut-proof glove,
thumbing its thumb at your plans

the helpdesk tech tells you to *get with* your
vending person, which today,
is you

you who can't ratchet your way out of a paper bag
who fears the mechanical maw
the copperhead chain drive
you who loves your intact hand
and sleek black jacket
befitting a midnight rider

you harken back to a simpler era
when children respected their elders
and coil machines unfurled themselves
dropping bags of chips
and glucose blossoms
into the aluminum tomb below—
a perverse reward at the end of the swim meet
after failing to make your heat

the old fart in stores
just grunts, asks you
when the hell it will be fixed

you build a cardboard cairn,
a four-corners monument of
unstocked product
outside the yard foreman's office
leave him the packing slip
as a postcard

Steve and I travel to Calgary

business casual: the uniform of confusion, which the engineers simply ignore. no one brings proper footwear. harried airport carnival, a carry-on cubic cram. a scheduled adventure, always with one unplanned pratfall. downtown—the tow truck, the cops. spring prying its delicate wrist from winter's grasp. open too late and closing too early. *where* is there decent coffee? something other than this faint solvent? we're also disturbed about bagels. where's my waitress? some beds are better than others, but none of them ours. generally, people are collegial. the continuous hum of conversation, conditioning the air. an accordion of topics. the view tends not to vary—mostly the headless semi-trailer caterpillars in sheet-metal *rigor mortis,* arrayed in a grid in the yard next door. the branch, located in the corner pocket—well clear of the ring road. which industrial strip mall? such dust. short walk to get the hell off our duffs. April—and the icy clots, crystal tourists thronging the thrombotic Bow River—are outrunning us. talk of people who had cancer and died. early dinner at the German deli, the airport security anaconda. the relief valve of mild complaints. the ceaseless announcements concerning the endless delays. the shuttle bus, the long-term parking lot that spits your keys out, the tired drive home.

big sale

nothing like a Monday morning where you wake up and before you get out of bed, you've sold a pump worth 100k to people whose process you know nothing about. happy Monday indeed. POs—those thunder eggs—stud your inbox. you send the round of exclamatory emails to the heavy lifters on the inside. not even the weekend's marital strife can strafe your high-flying ambitions, punch holes in your gleaming ultralight hull. you'd celebrate but, hey, Monday, and nobody on the coast hammers down anymore because everyone fought the law long ago. anyway these days we're all dispersed fireworks—red, amber reflections boogeying along the dark shoals of the bay. instead, you do the things you did when you were a sad kid. things that don't take much dough. you take a walk on the seawall and eat a couple of slices of pizza folded shut, like the harried people in the movies—Brooklyn-style, capicola flaccidly clapping. you're in a part of town you don't have time to get down to anymore, on a bench on the waterfront on the last gasp of a warm fall day, alone.

the test

Friday, five o'clock somewhere comes the email from the white whale, red exclamation mark a cyclopean poker. thus begins the weekend procurement circlejerk. a talus of loose ends—a Sisyphean quest for toilets, hot-water tanks, lockers, two hundred rolls of tinfoil, bunkbeds—shit we don't even sell. purchasers have their own special siren song: *I hate the other guys, and you guys have never let us down.* you'd've cracked a beer half an hour ago, but you've been driving a desk all day, so there is none. if Old Mother Hubbard were an alcoholic, she'd be hooped—a supply chain chump, washed up. this is the antithesis of sales guys golfing on a Friday afternoon. the insurers have made us such a bunch of churchgoers these days. no way in hell can you be the bottleneck on this one as you motorboat your way through this wheeler-dealer Strait of Messina. you call your manager, who tells you to call Brian, who's on call, who says to call Donna. Donna just laughs, because that's what Brian does. thanks a pantload. um. headscratching, googling—you tepidly offer Donna's suggestion of lame-o Home Despot, with the disclaimer that their toilets are probably not seaworthy, like the ones on the ferry. yeah, ask not for whom the bell tolls.

these are the guts (postcards from Mitchell Island)

these are the guts
neat lumber jenga
aggregate dunes
alembic sawmills
laddering themselves into thin air

arrow shipyard's marine lift sits,
marionette chains and thick slings
waiting to cradle ailing boats

dead-end rest stop—scrap land
scribbled with a wild rosebush
and two craggy picnic tables
gripping the north arm

ready-mix trucks shuffle along
to keep the dust down
drums orbiting right round,
brewing grey dough

crane spines collapsed, stacked
beside seacan Battenberg cakes,
staid neighbours to the clattering
marabou stork shears
that accordion ferrous bones

this civic bivalve garburator remains
the voice of precarious reason
filter-feeding
this ravenous city

sand & gravel

refining conveyors
teeth and tongues
sift, screen and
spit out

a shell, a shovel game
a Permian pawn interred in a wall
garden rods
construction cones
pea gravel
in a stone gunslinger

laying down the lawn

the earth's loamy crumbs
slip through our fingers
become pressed crust
under the stored cargo's sleek concrete
the forklifts skate along on

tilt-up stonehenges
line the dirty boulevard
lithe teen trees wave, flutter
light-industrial pageant contestants
sashed in orange flagging tape

fear and probability

here,
a woman's soft body
is found only
in cubicle fabric nests

but I am a huntress
sparkles under steel toes
shuffling between petrochemical rainbows
into open bays
under heavy-lift ulnae
along the riverfront

deliberately lost daily
I fear being found
a gutted freebird
floating greyly
against the boom chains

dig in

for Jónína Kirton

learn to become lignin
living, but stiff
the interdependent men
will talk
over you
at you
about you
object, topic

nascent agent

put your roots down
and pretend

the storms are normal

your tissues will
become inflamed by
the fine salt spray
of casual abrasions

you will be scarred by lightning indignities

the fight's a grind
each quiet ring
each arthritic old limb
a lonely, lovely victory

iron shirt 鐵衫

for Vince

the study
of high-gloss xylology
of marquise-scarred cordovan bark
occurs Sundays among the elm throng behind city hospital
where jonesers wait for their splintered bench connections

we stare through tennis courts and highrises
into our blind spots
peel century egg egos
into the imaginary bowls of our forearms

you came on as café fog
crema and steam teaching me
the business of heavy blows from
our morning orange moon's methane rain
a strike-anywhere reminder of being

born in the switchblade winter to
become a plum blossom woman

they canned a good man today

for Super J

first thing Monday—a hydrogen zeppelin of political dogshit. your office stripped of its Habs memorabilia. we can't find you. some back-east jackass flies in to finger-gun us while we burn. they canned a good man today. left your bereft flock in the pleather desert, marooned in the boardroom of the sweathog branch during a plague, a heatwave and a price war—it was a corporate apocalypse with ashen spectators. your splintered protégés suddenly rudderless. we sit—fishes eviscerated, fidgeting over your dead body, and this stable genius asks us *how we feel about this*. we are treated to his greasy megalomania over industrial-park Szechuan takeout on a vacant shop floor. frothy jocularity, boorish erasure. fake laughs and nominal notetaking in this Kool-Aid cavitation. let's circle back to lunacy (hell, let's spiral down): delusions of dystopian datafication/how he cleverly hid assets from his ex-wife/his backcountry derring-do (portaging a canoe solo somewhere among the blackflies)/his MBA. *we thank him for his service and wish him luck with his future endeavours.* all I know is shit runs downhill and payday's Friday.

the reincarnators (scrapyard)

steel starflower hooks—
you have revealed the beauty
in our twisted hulks
in our broken bones;
kindling in your
Sennebogen King Kong claw

you cannot step like the Jain
for the gods among men have already killed us for
their sport
their electronic decay
their dealer market

these fields bury the nails
and the acicular chrysotile
your friends warn you about

and here are the men with
bright eyes
and slowly eroding
hands

and the professional seeker
keeps walking through
this western valley of death
offering coffee and
mushroom clouds

sunset crew

get off the tools.
put down your metric wrench
and emerge from under
that shit-caked belly pan.
flush the grit from your eyes.

the world needs you,
eats you
after hours
every day it can

doctor and saint
deus *et* machina
of quonset monasteries
lock-block altars
and gravel pastures

they call you to attend
to the sputtering and dying;
goldenrod iron
whose four-wire arteries
are stiff with foreign ions

every day your ribs ache
and you remain,
turning the Riesenrad

they would call you into your eighties
if they could—
a greybeard coach in a twill shopcoat
whose sons have wandered away—

still weighing in,
still gardening stunted city kids

parts run

the industrial stop-and-go
the old in 'n' out
daily pockets of waiting
as a courier of
rubber veins
and steel elbows
for weeping machines

the parts counter—
a sort of standing mechanics' lounge
friendly hellos, and sideways eyes
for the woman with teal tile nails
it's worse in tank top weather—
a few drown in the pitcher plant of her cleavage

then back on Hwy 1
AC/greasy snarling
about high and hard living

sitting, spine calcifying, one bead in the pain-chain
weaving itself together onto the bridge

then speed—
slowing only for the RCMP pit vipers
hiding past the curves,
while mentally mapping the pinball traps
of previous tickets

she's a tiny dancer, a drive wheel
geared up in steel-toed pointe
and neon orange torso
rolling into the yard

with vulcanized organs
and a double-double
for the dirty surgeon

double box-end 60° offset
41–46 metric wrench

elusive.
were Dalí kayaking to work
on a river of fire
this would be his trusty paddle
odd copper-beryllium body
wrists twisted at angles from a Bangles' song
flames flowing through
dodecagon dahlia sockets

the inconsistency of memory
the persistence of a fucktonne of tasks

like this internet search,
going nowhere

if only you were
shorter
straighter
shallower—
standard.

work gear in the back of a truck cab

Two hi-vis vests. A good one, with too many pockets, and heavy as a horse blanket in summer. A beat-up one for a friend. The male version of the extra tampon, perhaps.

A sports bag that has barfed its contents of PPE everywhere.

Many sweaty socks—synthetic tumbleweeds slumped and crumpled under the jumpseat.

Safety goggles that suck the glasses off your face like an off-gassing, plastic lamprey. Attractive.

A hammerhead shark respirator mask. Just two red SOS pads between you and silicotic purgatory.

Coveralls strong enough for a man but made for a woman. You have nothing to lose but a bunching crotch and a hooking hazard.

Steel-toed boots blessed with lime dust by the high-priest of the bucket elevator. Every week it's Ash Wednesday. Penitence is the sentence of coughing up blood every morning. No one knew anything about this kind of shit back then.

grain terminal

for Evan

high above the black inlet
quick shimmering glimpses
snatched through a cracked asterisk
on sepia glass

two reps check a section of
steel rotini for
the new spine
on a screw conveyor

the grain terminal—
a tomb where the living
are milled to dust
to raise a new set of ghosts
across the ocean

colossal concrete
cannelloni xylophone silos
gibbous in the peripheral vision of the bridge

tug snouts, red rubber bull terriers banking
the freighters
into their berth

the shiploader
a spiny green sheet-metal crab
disperses pulses into vessels

double-Dutch staircases
sombre ultramarine
against varsity yellow
industrial trellises
ratcheting into hard sky

on the fourth floor
a gearbox slowly bleeds its contaminated plasma
into a limp cloud of rags

blasting accident

countdown to ka-BOOM!
rock face becomes crumbs

dynamite's diatomic dope
and slick nitroglycerin in
pallid thermoplastic sticks
make a handy bundle of megajoules
expand by mighty coefficient

galvanic mishap—the blasting cap flips off
a couple of the mining engineer's fingers,
and flings his iron ring in the misfire

car pad

in this urban charnel ground,
bobcat phlebotomists come as
high priests of salvage, these greasy rogyapas
with their grappling hook censers
prepare the scrap car, strip its ligaments
for its jacked-up sky burial

from the underbelly,
they drill holes in its steel glands
no pomp, they just pump
the bilious coolant, sallow oil
industrial blood through
accordioned intestines into tanks

bleed out all its road trips,
drunken doughnuts,
eviscerate its near misses and
leave its sheet metal storyless

boomtown

we are all just visitors here
in this concrete gasoline garden
good and evil are
unearthing second chances behind an ATCO trailer
folding them into bunkhouse bust hands
and burning them up

pipe dreams
lean young men become
gods galvanized in the crude Medusa machine

in Canadian tuxedos
and stubbled acceptance
in leaving their audience
of marginal farms and perennial girls

shuttered

everyone's now at the age where you only go back up for funerals. before Dirtbag's wake, you send me a photo of a quiet engine, a town without mitochondria. the old mill sags past its chain-link veil. security was the building with the blue facing. paper machines #5–8 down the hill and to the left. #9–11 back and to the right. smoke and steam all bled out, working-age population dissipated to the bigger smoke. not even a whisper of previous vibration. the young years you spent in the doghouse whenever #10 wasn't haying out, drinking coffee and staring at the grey while dreaming of a world beyond its walls to prevent the black liquor stranding your mind while the money rolled in. the six a.m. horn, that industrial muezzin, would sound the corporate call to labour and the dayshift's legion of guys in Campbell River dinner jackets would shuffle down the hill to deliver the world its blank page.

rig veda

track-drive giraffes
congregate by the Fraser
these saffron rigs,
speculation's unicycles,
are a practical saddle
for vaulting men's ambitions

towering hammerheads
driven by their kinematic backs
the Kelly bar carousel spins,
bar to the beat of the bushing
as the soil mixing mandalas'
black hole suns rotate,
make concrete pastry
with the broken riverbank
and the shards of this parcel's
previous incarnation

the diesel gearbox roars its boring hymn
for forward motion
an impermeable foundation
a monument to hard-assed risk
a prayer for a farm's erasure
for a city of empty glass sockets
with electronic ocularity
at every lit intersection

if: prey,
then: huntress

the worst thing you can do
is to talk to a man
like another man would

lead in with your chin
a pseudofonzarelli—
ayyyy!—one a theeese

split beaver as
tiki-head lanterns
crawling up the walls
hanging off the shipyard lunchroom
trawling all arms of the river

we two women in here
looking down
obliquely
and can't admit
to being foreign exchange students

guests in our own homes

we can excavate the crawlspace
like nobody's business

and we can hunt and gather—
so long as we keep
moving
laughing
forgetting

ACKNOWLEDGEMENTS

I liken the poetry ecosystem to a mangrove forest—composed of a dense tangle of prop roots that make the trees appear to be standing on stilts above tidal waters, protecting the shoreline and providing an oyster habitat.

Much gratitude to the poets below (including my teachers and friends) who provided habitat so that I could form my own nacre:

Pierrette Requier, Calvin Wharton, Mary Burns, Norman Nawrocki, Robert Colman, Jim Johnstone, Peter Norman, Fiona Lam, Evelyn Lau, the Harbour Centre 5, Kate Braid, Tom Wayman, Anne Simpson, rob mclennan, Jónína Kirton, Kevin Spenst, Leanne Boschman, Robin Susanto, Daniela Elza, Bonnie Nish, John Barton, Jen Currin, Raoul Fernandes and Kyeren Regehr.

Numerous poems in this book were previously published in the following literary journals (and anthology): *The Antigonish Review, Arc Poetry, EVENT, The Fiddlehead, Grain, The Malahat Review, PRISM international, Vallum* and *Best Canadian Poetry 2023*. Thank you to the editors.

Many thanks to Silas White, Janine Young, Fernanda Viveiros and your colleagues at Nightwood Editions.

Finally, thank you to my husband Paul, and to John Lamb for plenty of sparks for my works and days.

ABOUT THE AUTHOR

Photo credit: Steven Kirby-Schwartz

Christina Shah lives in New Westminster and works in heavy industry, where she drinks from the firehose of knowledge. Her poetry has appeared in numerous Canadian literary journals. Her work has been shortlisted for *The Fiddlehead*'s 2021 Ralph Gustafson Poetry Prize and has appeared in *Best Canadian Poetry 2023*. She is one-fifth of the Harbour Centre 5 poetry collective, whose chapbook, *Brine*, was released in 2022. Her first videopoem, "rig veda" (in collaboration with videographer Mark Mushet), was translated into Spanish and screened internationally. *rig veda*, her first solo chapbook (Anstruther Press), received an honourable mention for the bpNichol Chapbook Award in 2024. *if: prey, then: huntress* is her first full-length poetry collection.